About the Author

Line Andrea Johnsen is from Norway, and has been exploring creativity all her life. From dancing, theatre, singing and to the true craft in her heart, which is writing. She has one son, and runs her own little company in Trondheim. From time to time, she also works offshore in the North Sea. There has been a lot of moving around in Norway, and she also lived in Athens, which has been a huge inspiration for her writing.

Photo credit: Elise Johnsen

A Broken Heart, Soon to be Healed

L. A. Johnsen

A Broken Heart, Soon to be Healed

Olympia Publishers
London

www.olympiapublishers.com
OLYMPIA PAPERBACK EDITION

Copyright © L. A. Johnsen 2021

The right of L. A. Johnsen to be identified as author of this work has been asserted in accordance with sections 77 and 78 of the Copyright, Designs and Patents Act 1988.

All Rights Reserved

No reproduction, copy or transmission of this publication may be made without written permission.
No paragraph of this publication may be reproduced, copied or transmitted save with the written permission of the publisher, or in accordance with the provisions of the Copyright Act 1956 (as amended).

Any person who commits any unauthorised act in relation to this publication may be liable to criminal prosecution and civil claims for damage.

A CIP catalogue record for this title is available from the British Library.

ISBN: 978-1-80074-129-4

This is a work of fiction.
Names, characters, places and incidents originate from the writer's imagination. Any resemblance to actual persons, living or dead, is purely coincidental.

First Published in 2021

Olympia Publishers
Tallis House
2 Tallis Street
London
EC4Y 0AB

Printed in Great Britain

Dedication

To all out there that have, or are suffering in love, you have to feel feelings, before they are gone. Then there will be a new tomorrow.

-1-
A broken heart, soon to be healed

Why do we read sad stories and listen to dark music, when we are hurting?
Why does it feel better, and why do we do the opposite to our children?
We play cheerful music, and lift their spirit.

But our complex soul need its own time to heal. No matter what it is, that is pushing us down.

Life is both. Dark days, and those glorious moments of joy.
But when we are down, it is soothing to know that we are not alone.

L.A.J.

-2-
Fading

My memory of you is fading
still I'm blue.
Even though you don't want me,
I'm staying true.

You don't know that I'm burning inside,
you don't know that I'm hiding.

In your mind, I'm just someone you knew,
someone who loved you,
and always stayed true.

The trust you learned, in my company
made you blossom, made you free.
I loved you only, and would always stay.
The trust was not enough, not your vision,
not your way.

All the promises, when I needed to go.
All the tears, you wanted me to know.

That there was love, not now,
but forever.
You made me weep, when you said,
I was so much better (than you).

How could you be good enough,
how could you give me all?
I did not want what you could not give.
You were already my star.

Your soul I loved, but never could I stay.
You gave me hope when you begged me to stay.
But never could you love me now, later yes,
some love, somehow.

-3-
Weak

I don't recognise the kindness in your eyes
that I used to see.
When you kissed my cheek,
I crumpled, did not breathe.

The sparkle is gone,
so is the one you used to be, to me.
Loving, caring and in harmony.

Gone is the smile, when you grabbed my hand.
Little did I know, you wanted another …
Promised me a lifetime of joy,
but made me feel like a toy.

Gone are the nights we lay close,
the time we both had a choice.
the scent of you.
In the moment, I don't know what to do.

Will I ever love again? please tell me when.
The pain is numb,
I don't feel the hurting like I thought I would.
The way they say I should.

It never felt this way, all the times in the past.

It was a pain for a moment, like a blast.
Now my hope is for you to love me again,

My weak heart fools me to believe
that you always
will be more than a friend.

-4-
No more

You say you don't need me,
or my love, anymore.
You say that you don't want me,
to be near you no more.

All I sacrificed for you
all the years I held on to,
the thought of what we could have been.
So sad I could not win.

My gut kept screaming,
let my heart be left alone.
My shoulder carried
a load full of stones.

They almost broke me,
until you made me go.
I left, so sad,
but how could I know?

The love you never felt
for me, you see,
I knew all along.
That you wanted to be free.

But the feelings for what we could
have been together
made me forget through this rain
and stormy weather.

I still keep you in my fantasy,
where you love me
unconditionally.

-5-
Unreal

If it never was love
how could it be, that the sea
whispers your name
with every wave?

Like the gentle touch of your hand,
I feel your passion, feel your flame.
It heals me, completes me.
with every heartbeat,
when the waves whisper your name.

If it never was real,
your breath against my neck?
Your strong arms around my waist.
Someone I continue to chase.

If it was for ever,
would I care about this rainy weather?
Where my tears melt into eternity,
where you exist, feeling incompletely
without me.

If the future is without you,
why is there a light in my darkness,
where you forever have access?

Why do I still believe that you
are the one to release me?
The one with whom I'm supposed to be,
and forever stay and hold on to,
forever me and you.

-6-
Rejection

You did not want this forever,
I misunderstood.
On our journey to another level,
little did I know
it wasn't we, or forever.

Together was not in your vocabulary.
you wanted to travel,
you wanted to be free.
I blame myself, that I did not see.

Feelings of lust and rejection,
every day, I worked to dazzle
your election.
Sometimes you let me win,
in this blameful game of sin.

I flew high above of love.
All you did was to make sure
to let me know
that we would, maybe, never be
together on this journey, in symmetry.

I blame myself, I did not listen
and wasted all those years.

Every night without you,
my eyes were flowing with tears.

I don't want to blame myself
Anymore.
Even though it's still sore
I feel the love I felt, in a way
Even though you did not stay.

-7-
Worthless

I'm feeling worthless,
even though I'm loved.
But it's not flowing from the one
that made me feel this way.
Not by the one that did not stay.

There is no more I'm sorry,
cause you left in a hurry.

I'm aching after eternity
or at least
knowing I'm not all this shitty.

I begged you to stay true,
I was ready to give you my all.
If you said jump,
I would reach for the stars.

All I managed was to fall,
never did you catch me,
never did you watch me.
Pushed me to the wall.

Scared of the future
you once promised me.
Instead you let me go,
into the dark eternity.

-8-
Believed

For a weak moment,
I believed.
For a weak moment,
I thought I was healed.

How many of us
are broken,
with our feelings
left unspoken?

I'm feeling done,
no one has won.
I have nothing left to give,
I no longer feel the thrill.

No one believes me.
In their eyes I can see
that it hurts them
that I no longer believe.

There is nothing else
I need to do.
I just want to breathe.
I can never be with you.

-9-
Broken

All that was expected,
all that I believed.
By no one I was affected
only by myself, in whom I believed.

The claw in my gut
burned into my surroundings.

My struggle in love
is becoming a disease.
I can't sleep, I can't breathe
please give me release.

The tension between us,
all out in the open.
No one saw
that we both were broken.

Two hearts with different rhythm,
pretending being in tune.
It must have been so hard,
being you.

Someone who gave you love,
all this love that

did not cling to your soul.

All this confusion.
So we both left,
me broken,
with old scars, still open.

-10-
Fallen hope

Nothing of who I am,
deep inside,
is something you want
me to reveal, just hide.

All the questions you did not ask.
I was bursting out,
from time to time.
You expect me to keep on my mask.

Your laughter
when you for a moment
understood my soul.
And then, the joyful moment
was gone.

Your smile
when I didn't think you could stay.
You said
we just needed to lay.

Deep in your arms,
without anything in between.
Wonderful adventure for our souls,

for us to seal.

For a moment I believed in us,
a relation we could grow in joy.
Hours later I remembered,
you just play and act like a boy.

Nothing matters in daylight,
days are for fights.
Nothing is for our future,
cause there is nothing we, you see.

My heart shut down,
and slowly breaks.
All those wasted memories,
all those wasted days.

-11-
Broken dreams

You are no longer in my dreams,
they are all in ruins.
Broken windows and darkness,
hoping to survive this emptiness.

All I wanted was your embrace,
to touch and see your face.
Even though it's only a dream,
only on you I can lean.

Comfort me and dry my tears,
whisper away all my fears.
I don't really care
if it's going to take all year.

Where did you go,
don't you feel my love anymore?
The love is growing stronger,
even though I know it's over.

My distant memories
are painful in my dreams.
So why is the pain still here,
when I can't find you anywhere?

You broke my heart,
and now you are happy alone.
While I'm still missing you,
even in my dreams you're still gone.

-12-
Let me rewind

A blessing from someone
you never really knew.
Do you believe that is important?
Do you believe that is true?

A process of healing,
with memories burning in my mind.
Leave me alone
and let me please rewind.

Let me start all over again,
let me begin this journey
as a friend.

As your friend I would step back,
and never let you in.
I would never take that kiss,
and I would never let you win.

I would realise that you
would never love me
deep and true.

Freedom is the power
of your soul.

You are never serious
with females wanting your love.

Being at the wrong place,
becoming someone you always
had to chase.

Let me walk away from moments
you begged me to stay.
As a friend I would see
that you don't suit me.

I stay with you and observe
that the life you live
is not for me to occur.

Friends and not unspoken,
then we still would be unbroken.

-13-
The moment

Hopeful at your door
my beating heart,
waiting for a fresh start.

Secretly broken,
but faking strong.
I don't understand,
what I'm doing wrong.

The night-time in your arms
after 'don't go there' advice.
All that my body craves
is for you to call me babe.

You never spoke my name,
was that part of the game?

I'm longing to show you
how I feel.
That you are the one,
that my heart did steal.

You open the door,
a serious face.
Why did I not take that advice?

I feel empty,
and know I waste my time.
In that moment I understand,
that you will never be mine.

You almost fall into sleep,
while I struggle to fall out of you.
Again, I don't know what to do.

I try to hold you close to my face,
but you turn away
from my sweet embrace.

I'm no longer someone
you need to chase.
just someone to slowly erase.

-14-
Advice

All I know is fading away.
They say I will grow stronger,
these feelings will not stay.

Forget him and the love
he never felt.
You are so much better,
on a totally different level.

To me he was more, he was all.
Sometimes not enough,
and that was more than tough.

No one understands
that all I wanted
was for him to be my man.

His mind escaped all feelings,
even when he held me so close
I could hear his breathing,
wishing to be his choice.

Every day I wanted to
see him, feel him, with him stay.
But every day was not his way.

'Go out, don't you bother,
you will find another lover.'

-15-
Surviving

It will come a day
I no longer will feel this way.
No longer feel sorry,
honey, don't you worry.

What you see now is me,
aching and surviving.
Alone I escape
into my surroundings.

All I see is a life
I never thought I would have.
I truly once believed
I could have it all,
being loved by my only star.

I have to wait
for tomorrow.
Yesterday will never come back.
I have to believe
that my mind will be free.
Being complete without a 'we'.

-16-
Setback

I slowly remember
the lovely days.
Why I believed,
why I gave you my embrace.

I asked you once,
after months or a year.
To tell time's never easy,
being in love, when you're near.

Your body so warm,
how long will it be this way?
Forever, you said,
no reason for me not to stay.

A rush into a mind
of relaxation.
A couple of days,
with total confirmation.

Until I asked you again,
when the question was mine.
All I wanted then
was only to wine and dine.

You said I was asking for
too much of your time.
My heart dropped slowly,
removing the peace of my mind.

-17-
Bright Light

In the dark I'm free,
when I no longer believe.

Broken, but still alive.
What to learn
when all I want to do is cry?

All with you I did not want,
it's gone forever.
We will never again
see each other.

Not as a friend, not as a lover.
I understand that this is over.

I turn around in my darkness,
leave the unknown behind.
For something inside of me,
even if I don't know what to find.

I choose to embrace
the love I have inside.
For the child I once was,
that has no reasons to hide.

I need to caress
a life worthy of love,
and happiness I guess.

The love you left me
in your hurtful soul
was not good enough,
but out of my control.

I need to forgive myself
that I did not believe
I deserved something better,
I could not on you lean.

-18-
Wasted love

The life you dreamed of
is not in harmony.
Unpowered and broken,
despite of leaving me.

Your fear of losing the freedom
and falling with me
made you weak,
is that what you want to be?

Love is not a prison,
but a creation of harmony.
Why did you destroy that?
What is your meaning of being free?

The thought of the future
made you sick and lose control.
Then why did you ever
work to make me fall in love?

-19-
Fragile

The raw passion of me
is all you need.
My obsession of us,
you gave me back my trust.

I don't care if anyone
ever will see
you finally being with me.

This passion between us
slowly grow.
Deeper, stronger, warmer.
Please, never let me go.

Alone I feel fragile,
my flow is running slow.
Did you say you'll
come back?
I never wanted you to go.

Hours of waiting feeling sick,
already missing you so.
Will you ever come back?
Did I say I need to know?

-20-
New stranger

A numb silence
breaks through the noise.
Did I really take the right choice?
All I can hear is your voice.

Soft but clear,
the silence makes me stay.
Do you see me?
Will you shortly come this way?

A scent of your perfume
flows gently in the air.
I wish I was closer,
I wish that I was near.

A sound of a woman,
is it a friend?
I don't want to turn around,
I just want to feel the scent.

I'm slowly forgetting
all of you that's true.
The silence is no longer there,
I believe it never was you.

-21-
Promises

I promise I won't let
your new love know.
How you broke me into pieces,
and in two moments
you were gone.

I promise I won't get mad,
not destroy that love
you suddenly now have.

You turn away from my words
when I need a release.
To overcome my obsession,
to again believe.

I will be gentle, I will not cry,
if you promise not to lie.
If you promise to tell me why.

Look at me, look into my eyes.
I am true, was never in disguise.

Tell me you became wiser.
Promise me you love her,
Because we will never meet again

To me, you're only a liar.

Maybe there was another
for you all along.
If I knew I wouldn't bother,
and waste all these tears on my own.

-22-
Shadows

The end of a journey
is sometimes a release.
But the hurtful travel
is not always the disease.

Your shadows were not
suppose to be
on this journey with me.

Moments of affection,
where I am the proud election.
You suddenly appear,
from where?

The joyful moment is gone,
where did I go wrong?
Wine and sun in our eyes,
sharing life advice.

I remember we were here together,
then in rainy weather.
We laughed, you told me
you always stay true.
'Especially with a woman like you.'

My joyful moment,
I need to go.
I don't want to hurt someone,
don't ask,
you don't want to know.

I leave with your shadow
in my mind.
And hope someday I will find
someone to trust and believe.
Together on a journey, you and me.

-23-
Alone

You leave me alone,
still I'm by your side.
Or behind you,
several metres at a time.

Nothing gives us pleasure any more,
when we are alone.
And that is all I am with you,
Unpowered, not the one.

These crazy feelings do not
make sense.
They burn up my mind.
Give me a day this will end.

I want to relax in a soul
that is mine.
I don't want to waste any more
of my time.

-24-
Ungrowing

I see them everywhere,
like you, a true potential.
They themselves are not aware.

Not ready to commit.
Chaos in the mind
of who you are going to stay with.

The one you truly are,
create a mind full of war.

Talking to strangers,
doubting their truth,
holding on to your youth.

Working on those abs,
believe they will
give you a chance.

Why don't you develop your mind
and listen to your soul?
Maybe you then will believe,
Maybe you then will be whole.

You don't believe you are good enough.

You don't believe that it all has to stop.

In your chaos I was so close,
begging you to be mine.
But now I'm the one
that really doesn't mind
leaving you behind.

All the broken hearts
in the world.
I wish we could be free,
like the birds.
Come fly with me.

-25-
Breath

In the dark I'm free,
when I no longer
believe.

Broken, but still alive.
What to learn,
when all I want to do
is hide?

Craving for all I did not want,
believe that all love is over.
Or is there any left for my soul?
Is there anyone who will bother?

In my darkness I leave
the unknown behind.
Then maybe my heart
love will find.

I caress the love I have inside
for my inner child.
Self-worth, love and happiness
really have no limited age.

I believed a second chance

would be all that I need.
But it only created misery
in my heart I know that's real.

-26-
Stronger

Close to perfect but not enough,
you feed on my soul.
I'll tell you that is tough.

Why do you come here
and see me?
And why use your words
to defeat me?

You made it your choice
to be without me.
A confusion in my heart
when you beg for a fresh start.

Why do you cry?
I did not die.
I just left you on your own,
like the way you know.

The way you disrespected me
was too painful,
So I had to leave …

Feeling incomplete
without you here.

But my love was not enough
to comfort your fears.

A scar in our hearts
will eventually fully grow.
And there was love.
I know.

-27-
Gone

The days of
what I believed was your love
slowly disappear,
and soon they will be gone.

A blissful feeling,
where nothing is wrong.
For a moment I forgot
how it is to be strong.

The pain almost
became a part of me.
Waiting for some love
instead of setting myself free.

You don't exist in my life
anymore.
A memory is all I can think of,
that's for sure.

And in that weak memory
you tell me it's you.
Broken, bad and damaged,
now I believe that is true.

The tougher days
will maybe appear,
but at least I'm now aware.

That you never again
will be at my door.
My heart it will heal,
no longer be sore.

Forever never broken
by you.
That I know,
and that is my truth.

-28-
The choice

Heavy steps on my way home,
only moments before
I meet the unknown.

Lyrics of betrayal on my ear.
It soothes me,
removes some of my fear.

This moment will be
a bitter memory
one day, you'll see.

I know in my heart
that this answer
will rip out this potential start.

It will not become the joy and pleasure.
Not our in common treasure.

I'm seconds away from
being on my own.
I'm scared, but have no choice
but to welcome the unknown.

-29-
A new beginning

You reach out,
try to grab my hands.
Hope and love in your eyes.

I'm feeling safe when with you.
I'm sure you are kind and true.

But there's something in my gut,
I don't know.
Maybe because of the snow …

I'm shivering,
and exhale hesitating.
I wonder if you feel
this sudden worried tension.

You smile,
but slowly step back.
You understand
It's the trust I do lack.

The breeze of our summer is gone,
maybe I wasn't the one.

You reach out,

with your wonderful smile.
I smile back,
this emotion will take a while.

In trust I'll learn to blossom again.
But never, can I say when.

The sparkle in your eyes
is a genuine proof.
You will never tell me lies.
You will never me not choose.

Your patience needs to give me
some more time.
Maybe we need each other.
But first,
let's drink some more wine…

www.ingramcontent.com/pod-product-compliance
Lightning Source LLC
LaVergne TN
LVHW042002060526
838200LV00041B/1830